Dedicated to my wonderful children,
Chloe and Ben.

Thank you for the love, inspiration, and help,
that you have given me
to make Snoff come to life.

Snoff the Sloth

First published in the United Kingdom in 2018

By

Kdcrookes Publishing

Kevin Crookes has asserted his moral right to be identified as the author of this work.

All rights reserved.

No part of this book may be reproduced or transmitted in any form or by any means, electronic or mechanical, including photocopying, recording, or by any information storage and retrieval system without the express permission from the publisher.

Cover design and illustrations by Nicola Spencer

Copyright © Kevin Crookes

ISBN-13: 978-1987722918

SNOFF THE SLOTH

Written by Kevin Crookes

Illustrated by Nicola Spencer

Can you find the  on each page?

Snoff the sloth does not have paws. He has quite long legs and very long claws.

Snoff the sloth has a black nose.

On his feet, he has three short toes.

For his safety, in trees he is found.

Snoff the sloth has bright brown eyes.

He can be heard for miles when he lets out his cries.

One day Snoff could hear an inviting sound.

Risking danger to himself, he climbed down to the ground.

So when a leopard walked by he was hard to see.

He made his way to the water and started to swim.

He swam towards an island as quickly as a sloth could.

With him being in the water, danger was about.

There were sharks nearby and he needed to get out.

Snoff made it to the island and left the water behind.

The call was even louder, so off he went to find.

"EEEEEEE- AHH!"

He slowly moved forward and looked up to see.

The call was coming from a very big tree!

Snoff moved closer, trying not to make a sound.

He really was unsure of what could be around.

He climbed high up the tree with a big smile that beamed.

For there was the girl sloth of whom he had dreamed.

Fun Facts about Sloths

Sloths are a medium-sized mammal. There are two types of sloth the two-toed sloth and the three-toed sloth.

A sloth's body is usually 50 to 60cm long.
Sloths mainly eat the tree buds, new shoots, fruit and leaves.

Sloths are tree-dwelling animals, they are found in the jungles of Central and South America.

Sloths have a four-part stomach that very slowly digests the tough leaves they eat, it can sometimes take up to a month for them to digest a meal. Digesting this diet means a sloth has very little energy left to move around making it one of the slowest moving animals in the world.

Sloths move along the ground at just 2 m (6.5 ft) per minute! In the trees they are slightly quicker at 3 m (10 ft) per minute.

All sloths actually have three toes, but the two-toed sloth has only two fingers.

The sloth has very long, sharp, and strong claws that they use to hold on to tree branches. The claws are also their only natural defence against predators.

Sloths are tree-dwelling animals, they are found in the jungles of Central and South America. Sloths usually only leave the tree the live in to go to the toilet once a week on the ground.

It is believed that sloths sleep for around 10 hours a day.

In the wild, sloths live on average 10 - 16 years and in captivity over 30 years.

Kevin Crookes is a poet/author from Southampton in the United Kingdom who discovered a talent later on in his life for being able to make words rhyme.

So far he has written two poetry books called "AS IT IS" and "STILL AS IT IS" and two children's books called "Huxton the Hedgehog" and "Meo the Meerkat".

He began writing about seven years ago. One day, when he was walking along a beach, suddenly verses started to go through his mind in rhyme. He then decided that he should write some of these rhyming verses down so when he got home he took out a pencil and pad and started writing what he had been thinking about. Once he started writing he could not stop and the verses turned into poems. One poem turned to ten and so on and to date he has written over 300.

Over the last four years he has moved into writing children's books, which he really enjoys and has recently written more stories waiting to be published.

Follow Kevin and his ventures on his website at;

www.kdcrookes.com

Printed in Great Britain
by Amazon